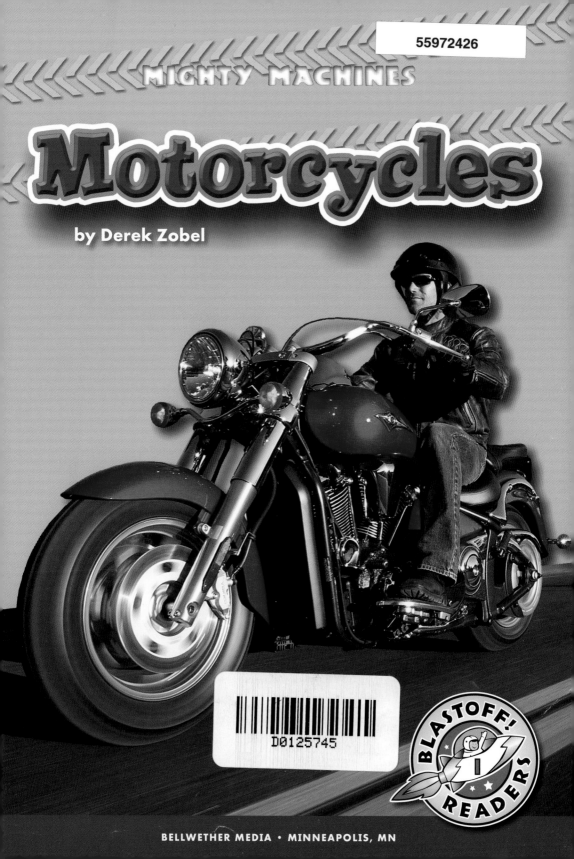

MIGHTY MACHINES

Motorcycles

by Derek Zobel

BLASTOFF! READERS

BELLWETHER MEDIA • MINNEAPOLIS, MN

Note to Librarians, Teachers, and Parents:

Blastoff! Readers are carefully developed by literacy experts and combine standards-based content with developmentally appropriate text.

Level 1 provides the most support through repetition of high-frequency words, light text, predictable sentence patterns, and strong visual support.

Level 2 offers early readers a bit more challenge through varied simple sentences, increased text load, and less repetition of high-frequency words.

Level 3 advances early-fluent readers toward fluency through increased text and concept load, less reliance on visuals, longer sentences, and more literary language.

Level 4 builds reading stamina by providing more text per page, increased use of punctuation, greater variation in sentence patterns, and increasingly challenging vocabulary.

Level 5 encourages children to move from "learning to read" to "reading to learn" by providing even more text, varied writing styles, and less familiar topics.

Whichever book is right for your reader, Blastoff! Readers are the perfect books to build confidence and encourage a love of reading that will last a lifetime!

This edition first published in 2010 by Bellwether Media, Inc.

No part of this publication may be reproduced in whole or in part without written permission of the publisher. For information regarding permission, write to Bellwether Media, Inc., Attention: Permissions Department, 5357 Penn Avenue South, Minneapolis, MN 55419.

Library of Congress Cataloging-in-Publication Data
Zobel, Derek, 1983–
  Motorcycles / by Derek Zobel.
    p. cm. – (Blastoff! readers. Mighty machines)
  Includes bibliographical references and index.
  Summary: "Simple text and full color photographs introduce beginning readers to motorcycles. Developed by literary experts for students in kindergarten through grade 3"–Provided by publisher.
  ISBN 978-1-60014-269-7 (hardcover : alk. paper)
  1. Motorcycles–Juvenile literature. I. Title.

TL440.15.Z63 2010
629.227'5–dc22   2009008275

Text copyright © 2010 by Bellwether Media, Inc.
Printed in the United States of America, North Mankato, MN.
021510   1159

Contents

A motorcycle is a **motor vehicle** with two wheels.

A motorcycle gets power from an **engine**. The engine is under the gas tank.

engine

Motorcycles have **handlebars**. Drivers use the handlebars to balance and steer.

handlebars

A driver turns a handlebar **grip** to speed up and slow down.

grip

This motorcycle has a **sidecar**. It carries a rider.

sidecar

This motorcycle has a **fairing**. It protects the riders from the wind.

fairing

A **scooter** is a small motorcycle. It works well in cities.

A **touring bike** is a big motorcycle. It is used to take long trips.

A **sport bike** is a motorcycle built to race. Watch it speed to the finish!

Glossary

engine—a machine that makes a vehicle move

fairing—a front part on some motorcycles that blocks wind

grip—a handle that a driver turns to control the speed of a motorcycle

handlebars—the tubes in front of a motorcycle driver; handlebars are used for balance and steering.

motor vehicle—a vehicle powered by a motor or engine

scooter—a small motorcycle

sidecar—a small car with a seat that is attached to one side of a motorcycle

sport bike—a kind of motorcycle built for speed

touring bike—a large motorcycle used for long trips

To Learn More

AT THE LIBRARY

Goodman, Susan E. *Motorcycles!* New York, NY: Random House, 2007.

Hill, Lee Sullivan. *Motorcycles.* Minneapolis, Minn.: Lerner, 2004.

Riggs, Kate. *Motorcycles.* Mankato, Minn.: Creative Education, 2007.

ON THE WEB

Learning more about mighty machines is as easy as 1, 2, 3.

1. Go to www.factsurfer.com.

2. Enter "mighty machines" into the search box.

3. Click the "Surf" button and you will see a list of related Web sites.

With factsurfer.com, finding more information is just a click away.

Index